The fox

It is a warm night in spring.
Four fox-cubs are playing in the moonlight.
They are having fun-fights with each other.
Their mother is not with them tonight.
She is out hunting for food, because the cubs
are not old enough to hunt for themselves.
The fox's home is called an earth.
One entrance is near the roots of a tree.
If danger threatens, the cubs will disappear
down the hole into the earth, and lie still,
waiting for the mother fox to return.
When the fox-cubs were born, they were blind
and helpless, and had no fur at all.
Vulpa, their mother, suckled them with her milk.
But now they are growing big and strong.
Soon they will be able to go hunting with her.

Vulpa the vixen, or mother fox,
has been hunting all night long.
She must find food for herself,
and for her four growing cubs.
So far she has been unlucky tonight.
She has eaten only insects and worms.
Vulpa stops and sniffs the air
with her wet, pointed nose.
She pricks up her ears and listens.
She can hear every sound in the grass.
Her eyes can see every movement.
As she crosses the damp grass, she makes
footprints, which smell of fox, in the soil.
Foxes have scent-glands under their tails,
and on the pads of their feet.
These give off a strong smell of fox.
She must hurry, because when it grows light,
the men with the dogs come out to hunt.

Vulpa the vixen leaps across a ditch,
and crosses a field where the new wheat is growing.
Suddenly she stops in her tracks.
She can hear something moving in the wheat.
Step by step, she creeps nearer to the sound.
Her body is ready to pounce,
and her jaws are ready to snap.
She has moved down-wind of the animal,
so that it will not smell her coming.
Now she will catch something to eat.

Foxes eat young rabbits and hares,
rats, mice, voles and shrews.
In this way, they help the farmer,
by ridding his land of pests.
But sometimes foxes become thieves.
They steal eggs from the hen-house.
They kill the farmer's chickens and ducks.
Sometimes they take the young lambs.
Farmers do not like foxes at all.
They often set traps to catch them.

When she comes nearer, Vulpa the vixen
sees a young rabbit nibbling at the wheat.
This is the sound she has heard.
Suddenly, she leaps into the air and pounces.
She snaps up the rabbit in her sharp teeth.
The rabbit dies at once.
Then Vulpa sets off through fields and woods
towards her distant earth.
The night will soon be over.
Her cubs will be very hungry.
It is time to return to her family.
As Vulpa runs, her ears are still pricked.
She listens for the sound of barking dogs.

For many hundreds of years
foxes have been hunted for sport,
and for their thick, glossy fur.
Men use special dogs to hunt foxes.
These dogs are called fox-hounds.
They are trained to follow the trail
of a fox for many hours at a time,
and across many kilometres of land.
But, in spite of their enemies,
foxes have survived.
They are clever animals, who are
skilled at covering up their tracks,
and at throwing the hounds off the scent.
Many stories have been written
about the cunning fox.
How many do you know?

A long way off, from behind some pine trees,
Vulpa can hear the barking of dogs.
The fox-hounds are out with their masters.
Now Vulpa must run for her life.
She darts through bushes and hedges,
and runs along dry ditches towards the woods.
This is her territory, and she knows it well.
She knows its secret paths and hiding places.
But the fox-hounds have found her strong scent.
They bark with excitement as they follow the trail.

A pheasant flaps up into the air
at the sight of a fox on the run.
All through the woods,
the noise of the chase can be heard.
The birds are afraid, and fly off.
But Vulpa the vixen is cunning.
She knows how to outwit
the hounds who are following her.
She must make haste,
because in the light of day
her reddish-brown coat shows up
against the green countryside.
If the hounds catch sight of her,
she will not stand a chance.

The hounds follow the smell of fox.
Their noses sniff the ground,
and their tails wave in the air.
They bark and whine as they run.
Vulpa the vixen makes her way to a stream
which flows through her territory.
She jumps into the cold water,
and swims down-stream for several hundred metres.
All the time, she still carries
the dead rabbit in her mouth.

On the bank of the stream, the hounds stop.
The trail has completely disappeared.
The stream has carried away the scent of fox.
The dogs splash about in the water,
but they cannot tell which way the fox has gone.
In the end, the huntsmen call off the hounds,
and go home for their breakfast.

When Vulpa is safe, she climbs out of the stream,
shakes her wet fur, and runs off through the woods
towards her waiting family.

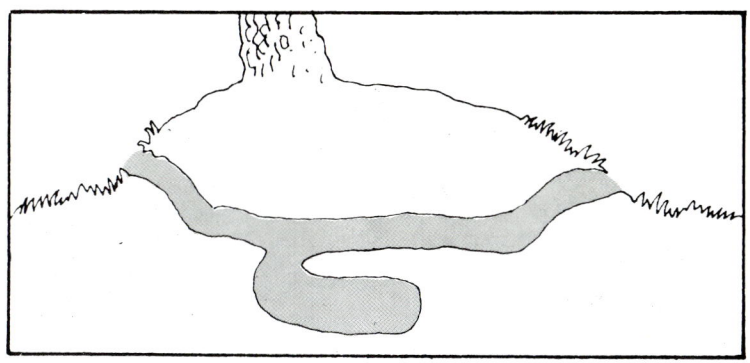

Vulpa the vixen arrives safely at her earth.
The hungry cubs run towards her.
They have waited a long time for a meal.
They tug at the rabbit in their mother's mouth.
When she drops it, they quickly pounce,
and gobble it up, leaving only a few bones.
Vulpa lies at the entrance to the earth and rests.
She is too tired to eat.
This time she has escaped from the hounds
and from the men who use dogs to hunt foxes.

Some facts about foxes

Vulpa the vixen is a red fox.
Foxes belong to the dog family,
which includes wolves and jackals.
Foxes are found all over the world.
The arctic fox lives in the far north.
The tiny fennec fox lives in deserts.
All foxes have a thick, bushy tail,
that huntsmen call a brush.
The male is called a dog fox.
The female fox is a vixen.
Each fox has its own territory,
which it marks with its scent.
The fox's earth has one main entrance,
and several smaller holes, or exits.
Foxes only make use of their earth
when they are rearing cubs.
The cubs are hidden for four weeks.
Then they begin to come out to play.
The vixen teaches them to hunt,
and to find food for themselves.
After six months, the cubs leave
their mother, and live on their own.
Here are some of the many things
which foxes eat. Can you name them?

Some of the fox's food

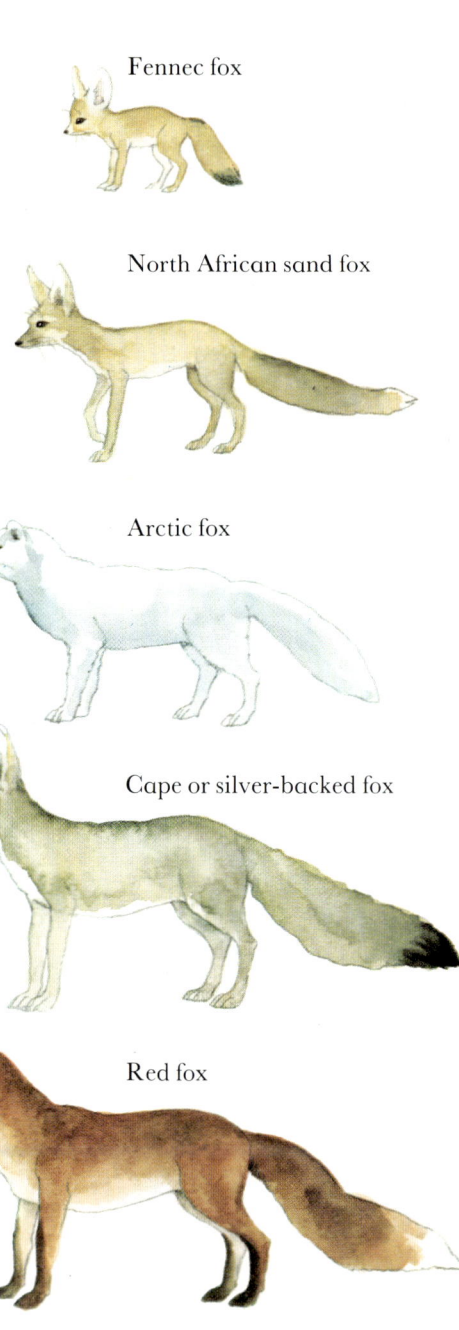

Fennec fox

North African sand fox

Arctic fox

Cape or silver-backed fox

Red fox